Shining Stars

by Marilee Robin Burton

illustrated by Amy Young

MODERN CURRICULUM PRESS
Pearson Learning Group

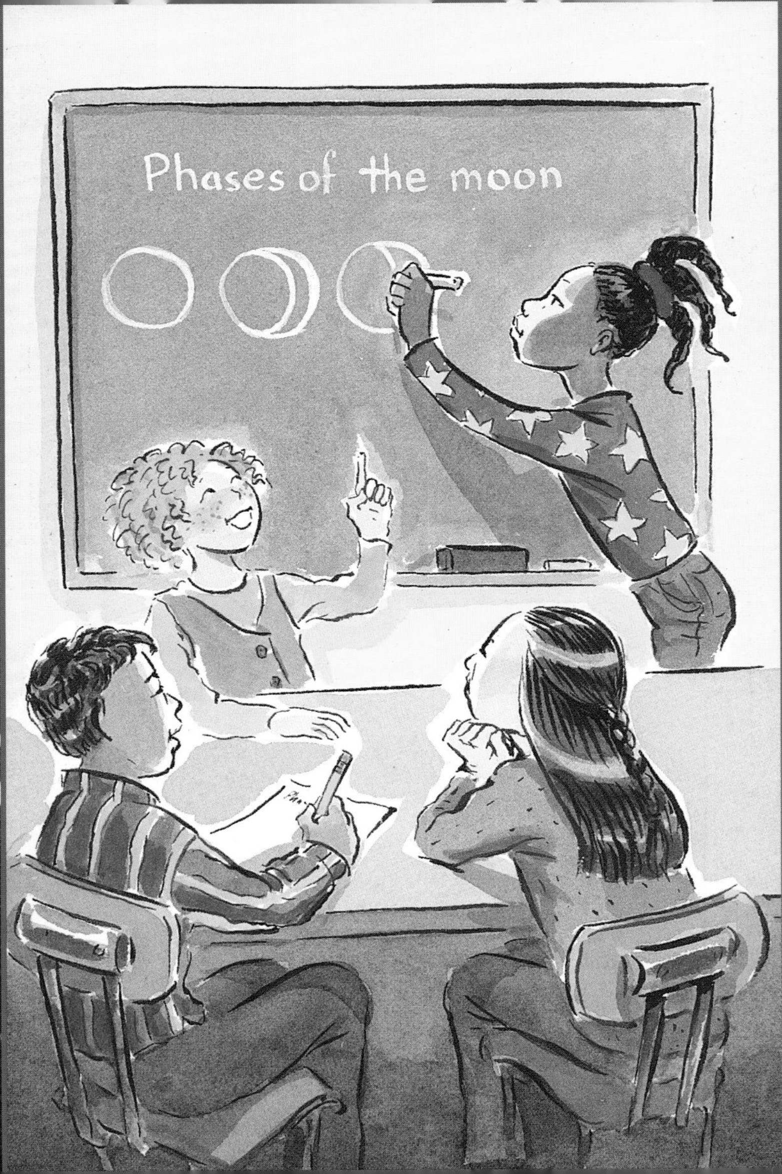
Phases of the moon

I used to be a star. I was a star in Mrs. Richard's sixth-grade class. Introducing *me*, Miss Jenny Jackson, the star, and my satellites: Pam, Sue, and Thomas.

Now I'm not conceited or anything. I love my friends and think they're all wonderful and have great qualities, but I've been fascinated by space and stars and the solar system forever. I know all about the constellations, galaxies, and space travel. Everyone knows Mrs. Richard is a big outer space fan, and she always has her sixth-grade class spend the whole year learning about what's millions of miles away. So I had an edge on everyone in my sixth-grade class, because I was already a serious space researcher.

When I was in the third grade, I wrote to NASA, the National Aeronautics and Space Administration, to volunteer to be the first space kid, if they were interested. I was sure my parents wouldn't mind my blasting off in a rocket, so I told NASA I could go as long as it was summer and I wouldn't miss any school. (My parents are big on the school thing.)

But they didn't have a program for kids in space yet, and so far, only grown-ups have gone along for the rocket ride. There are no suits or seats for school kids, but I'm still hoping I'll be the first someday.

Pam's dad was the first one to call me a star one day last October. We were going to meet at Pam's house to build a model of the solar system. I had the idea that we should include the moons of all nine planets—all sixty-one of them. Maybe we could even write some moon poems. I'd write about Io, because Io is so cool. Even its name is cool. *Eye-oh, eye-oh!* It sounds like a song. Io orbits Jupiter and is the only other space body in the solar system besides Earth that has volcanoes. Io erupts, which is pretty neat.

I was in the middle of thinking of words that rhyme with *Io,* when Thomas and Sue met me on the corner of Elm Street. "Io, Io, way up in the sky-o, you float by-o by-o, while I'm down here in Ohio." Pretty soon Sue and Thomas were adding verses too.

By the time we got to Pam's house and rang the bell, we had a whole song and chorus. When Pam's father opened the door, I was singing lead while Thomas and Sue chimed in on the moon chorus. "Well, if it isn't the star and her satellites!" Pam's dad had announced.

From then on we were known as "the star and her satellites." I was the space expert and everybody knew it, but that was all before Glenda Brown came to town.

Glenda's family came here the first week in March. Glenda seemed nice enough when Mr. Dolby brought her to our classroom.

She was quiet and a little shy, still everyone thought she was an okay kind of kid. Mrs. Richard gave her a seat next to Thomas, who showed her where we were in our science books. She started working right away, so no one even noticed her much at first. I know I sure didn't.

As soon as Mrs. Richard began a class discussion on our galaxy, though, Glenda's hand went sailing straight up. No matter what Mrs. Richard asked, Glenda's hand was high in the sky. She knew the answer to every question, and I mean *every* question!

Glenda knew that relative to other moons in our solar system, one of Jupiter's moons, Ganymede, is the largest. Glenda knew all about Io and that Venus rotates in a direction opposite to that of the other planets. Glenda knew that the astronaut's footprints on the moon could last a million years and that 25 tons of meteorite dust land on Earth each day. Glenda knew that the Milky Way has more than 100 billion stars in it. I mean, Glenda knew EVERYTHING!

Before long it was obvious to everyone that Glenda was the real space expert in our school. She was amazing. How did she know so much? That's when my star turned into a black hole, and you know, once a star turns into a black hole, it can't be seen. No light shines in a black hole, and that's exactly how I felt—cold and dark.

I felt as if no one saw me anymore. Once Glenda Brown walked into our sixth-grade class, she became the center of every orbit. Now she was the first person kids went to with any and every space question.

I had to do something about this, so I started to study harder than ever. I started to read more than ever, and I started to raise my hand more in class.

It was no longer my goal to be the first kid in space, or to know absolutely everything about the sixteen moons of Jupiter, or to be the Cedarville Elementary School space expert. Now my goal was simply to know as much about space as the amazing Glenda Brown. I wanted to be a star again, and that was the only way I knew how to do it.

So I studied and read, and studied some more. In fact, I was so busy studying, I didn't pay much attention to anyone. I sneaked in extra reading every chance I got, even at recess. I backed out of soccer games and read instead of playing doubles at handball. I ate, slept, breathed, and read.

I was scared kids would like Glenda more than me. I didn't want to lose my friends, but I was so busy, I didn't notice that no one paid much attention to Glenda at lunch or recess.

I didn't notice this until one day a meteorite landed in my lap, so to speak. I was reading outside after lunch while the other kids were busy running or tossing balls. Most were at soccer. I wasn't too interested in outside activities at that time, unless they involved the nighttime sky. Just then, in the middle of reading about Orion, the brightest constellation, Glenda turned up.

She spoke shyly and asked if she could sit down next to me, because she didn't want to run or play. Like me, she just wanted to read.

Well, I didn't really want her sitting next to me, but before I could think of a polite way to say no, Glenda immediately started talking, like one scholar to another. She told me how her family constantly moves around and how she's always the new kid at school. She told me how hard it is for her to make new friends, which is why she studies so much. She told me how she'd noticed I was always reading too, and maybe, she thought, we could be friends.

Suddenly it seemed as though Glenda's star wasn't in the middle of such a perfect constellation after all, and it didn't seem as if mine had turned into a complete black hole either. Maybe we *could* be friends after all. I could introduce Glenda to the other kids, and she in turn could help me study the sky. Besides, outer space is incredibly immense—there should be plenty of room for both of us. Maybe, just maybe, nobody is only a star, or only a satellite, all of the time.

"No, you can't sit next to me," I said, "not right now anyway." I stood up and grabbed her hand, pulling her to her feet.

I took her to the field, and I pulled her right into the middle of a new constellation—my satellites. This constellation would have a multitude of shining stars from now on, just like the Milky Way. It would, that is, if Jenny Jackson had anything to do with it.